THIS COLORING BOOK BELONGS TO

ooooooooooooooooooooooooooooooooo

ooooooooooooooooooooooooooooooooo

ooooooooooooooooooooooooooooooooo

www.ingramcontent.com/pod-product-compliance
Lightning Source LLC
Chambersburg PA
CBHW081237080526
44587CB00022B/3975